The Natural Self

By Rhonda Brandrick and Michéal Connors

All profits from this book go towards the social enterprise Human Nature to support people in deepening their connection to themselves, each other and the Earth.

ACKNOWLEDGMENTS

We would like to thank our teachers and mentors and guides, including Bill Plotkin, Geneen Marie Haugen, Mary Evelyn Tucker, John Grimm, Brian Swimme, and many others who continue to offer great guidance and support.

We would like to thank the Deane clan for their input as well and the wonderful illustrations they produced.

We would like to thank all of the people we have worked with who have offered us insights, wisdom and open-heartedness; work on the land has helped us shape this book. We continue to acknowledge the unfolding evolutionary story of the earth and universe that continues to shape who we are.

The Natural Self

By Rhonda Brandrick and Michéal Connors

© 2018 Rhonda Brandrick and Michéal Connors

ISBN 9781912092642

First published in 2017 by Arkbound Ltd (Publishers)

Cover image by Michéal Connors

Photography by Rhonda Brandrick

Illustrations by Lola Deane and Jenny Deane

Poetry by Rhonda Brandrick and Michéal Connors

Arkbound is a social enterprise that aims to promote social inclusion, community development and artistic talent. It sponsors publications by disadvantaged authors and covers issues that engage wider social concerns.

Arkbound fully embraces sustainability and environmental protection. It endeavours to use material that is renewable, recyclable or sourced from sustainable forest.

Arkbound
Backfields House
Upper York Street
Bristol BS2 8QJ
England

www.arkbound.com

CONTENTS

Section 1

Welcome

This book is offered as a way for you to deepen into a sense of yourself as an indigenous part of Earth. It comes out of many years of being on the land, working and engaging with people as they deepen their knowing of themselves, other people, and the wild earth.

We have been honoured to stand beside them as witnesses and guides, supporting them towards the deep resources of their Natural Self, its wisdom, resources and mysterious connections to earth.

In that time we have come to know that being in nature engages at all levels of the mind, body and soul. This connection to the natural world also reflects our true mysterious and awe-inspiring depths; in deep wonder we see our Natural Self mirrored in the stars, a blade of grass, or the wind blowing through the trees. We have clearly seen that being connected in the natural world brings forth a rich and transformational landscape full of potential healing, invitations to wholeness, opportunities and guidance on the initiation of our deepest purpose and soul.

It is apparent that within our dominant contemporary cultural story this indigenous connection to Earth has been lost, and is being further forgotten as we consume and dominate that which is home. It can be argued that this has led to fundamental isolation, trauma and even the roots of a collective madness. Thus we journey as modern human beings, often stumbling and falling, lost, hungry and thirsty for something natural and wild.

This book and journal is to be carried on the journey, to be a useful resource that can assist you in the remembering, re-imagining and re-wilding of your Natural Self. We offer it as a resource to help you re-engage with the dreaming of the earth and the cosmos, and to further find your place within the web of all things.

Within this book, and the journal incorporated, we encourage you to dive into the teachings, the practices, the land and the mythic realm where symbols, poetry and creativity can emerge and act as vessels of deep meaning and transformation.

Wild Blessings,

Michéal and Rhonda

An Invitation

We are more than we can ever know – more creative, more mysterious, more whole, more wild, and more connected.

Inside us all is the calling we long so terribly to hear: the calling of our deepest Natural Self and the connection to our soul.

This calling, at times heard in whispers in a gentle wind, howling gales, or the rustle of tiny creatures waking to the dawn.
This calling, felt in a single moment in sunlit groves, on skin bathing in the heat.
This calling, seen in a drop of rain falling from a leaf, in the shape of a cloud at sunset and in the movement of a blade of grass in the summer breeze.
This calling, felt in the beauty of the frost on bare trees.

Longing in our grief, we are waiting to hear it.
Longing in this soft grief, this wild grief, this torrent that washes through our hearts, opening us to our true possibilities.

If we dare to hear our calling, and feel the longing, then maybe more of our gifting will emerge, which we can offer to each other and to all of nature.

This gifting, once further extracted from the creative, mysterious darkness of our depths, offers new illumination on the unfolding of ourselves, humanity, other than human life, the earth, and the cosmos.

This gifting is not just an object, a single boon, but a journey – a journey that leads us through rough undergrowth and wild lands, soft meadows and gentle seas, guiding us in our healing, our becoming whole, and to the depths of the soul.

We invite you to dive further into this exploration, and begin to re-mind, re-body, re-wild and re-imagine who you are, in a natural life for you, each other, and the wild world that welcomes your remembering.

A Natural Self: Future ways from ancient paths.

Glossary

A Global Indigenous
We acknowledge the wonderful diversity of cultures across the world and honour them. We also see the emergence of the global human; one who senses connection to themselves as a part of a greater earth community and one who feels indigenous to the planet as a whole.

Natural Self
When human beings are in contact not only with their personal and social world, but connected deeply to their inner nature, and greater nature around them.

Holistic Ecopsychology
The study of the mind, body and soul as an aspect of earth and cosmos.

Participation with Earth
A way of being in the world where we know we are participating in a great evolutionary story in relationship to all things.

Reciprocal Relationship
Our human nature relationship is always in a reciprocal giving and receiving with the more than human world.

The More Than Human World
This includes the human experience but within the whole of life, Earth and cosmos.

Healing, Wholing and Ensouling
Our journey of becoming our natural self as we heal our fragmentation and wounds, embody what is whole in us and live into our deepest purpose and gifting.

Earth Community
All beings and ecosystems that constitute the natural world.

Inscendence
The journey of diving deeply into our Natural Self going deeply, into mind, body and soul. Facing the unknown and finding our hidden gifts.

The Natural Self

For many years, a dominant human culture has sought to discount our relationship to our inner Natural Self and our indigenous connection to the land. This has been driven by many historical factors that are not within the scope of this little book. However, this has left many of us struggling deeply in ourselves, with each other and in a world where the destruction of our natural environment and the earth's wild habitat continues.

The disconnect from our natural selves has led to a deepening psychological, environmental and spiritual crisis in the personal and human collective. This fracture from our fundamental selves and our home is, as Chellis Glendinning states, the 'original trauma' (1), sometimes leading to an ever-increasing need to fill our lives with addictions, drama and dis-ease that fog up the emptiness we can feel when the deep, natural connections to self, others and the earth are not present.

Common experiences may include:-

- Disconnect from our bodies and our fundamental inner nature
- Disconnect from our home, the local land and the earth
- A singular self-oriented view of life
- Materialism and consumption as the primary purpose of life
- Creativity as something only for entertainment and consumption
- Human needs and desires dominating
- Over-reliance on our intellect as a way of knowing
- The loss of the sacred relationship to mystery
- A disconnect from our ancestors and our future ones
- The creation of a disconnected ego that seeks fulfillment in material wealth and consumerism
- A sense of isolation and loss of community both with our human kin and the other than human community
- A disconnect from our soul, spirit and our sense of place in life
- Despair and depression

One of the big questions that follows is: *What can we do? How can we begin to rediscover ourselves and our communities within a deeper connection to our self, each other and nature?*

For many, it is time to come back to our Natural Selves and to each other in Earth-supporting cultures. Across the world, projects, communities and individuals are finding ways of living that are in greater balance and harmony – creative ways of living that encourage deeper connections to the self, others and the Earth.

For these new ways of living to flourish, this book offers some ideas, teachings and practices that we know will support the recovery and thriving of our Natural Selves and the emergence of a Global Indigenous.

It is also time that we acknowledge this global nature of our presence, and the responsibility for our biome that comes with it. We know that a life dedicated to the practices we offer, and other Earth-connecting methods will allow us to rekindle our full human potential, and rediscover our place as an integral part of the web of life. In this recovery and flourishing we can become the guardians of our sacred and mysterious Earth, and the Earth Community that we are part of. We want to find ways of enlivening what Thomas Berry talked to so passionately as 'the great work' (2).

So let us look at some of the fundamental aspects.

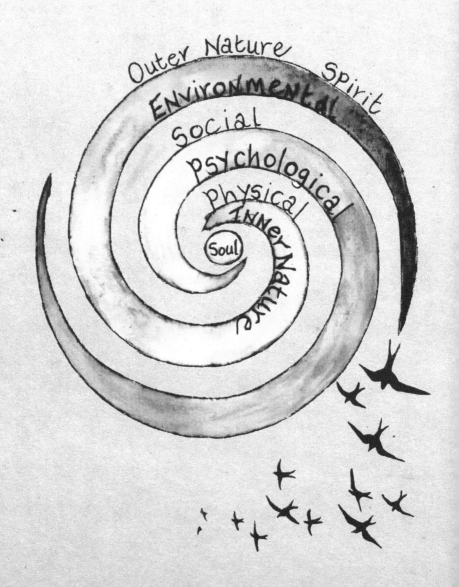

Outer Nature
Spirit
Environmental
Social
Psychological
Physical
Inner Nature
Soul

Figure 1

The Natural Self Model

We know that any model is always a simplification and that any map is not the territory. Given that, we are seeking to offer you support, ideas, discernments and lenses that may help you experience, feel or see more of your own natural self and your connections to the natural world around you. Throughout this book we talk about the Natural Self, and point to an approach to developing this further, encouraging us to live in ever-deepening contact to our inner nature, deepest purpose (soul), body and mind.

Within this approach is also an acknowledgement of the need to build an Earth-focused human community in harmony with the environment, and connected to the bigger story of Earth and the cosmos.

This approach is represented by the image below. We know that it is only that – a map, and not the territory, which in reality is both interdependent and connected, but we find this to be a useful way of showing what we mean by the Natural Self.

- Throughout the model is nature which is fundamental to our life and instincts; the wild and mysterious centre is our connection to our individual, unique part in the whole. This can also be seen as the place of soul. Bill Plotkin states, "by Soul I mean the vital, mysterious and wild core of our individual selves..." (3).

- Next is our body as it grows into a sensitive, feeling, physical experience of the world around us, offering us the wisdom of the felt-sense and the ancient evolutionary process that created it.

- We then represent the mind and all that is within this: our psychology, personality – both the fragmented aspects and the wholeness – as well as a gateway to the imagination

- We are in a relationship to people, and so the next level is our human community.

- Then, the environment we live in, which for many of us is urban.

- And finally, outer nature, which encompasses the greater nature of Earth and the cosmos, and the expansive connection to all – this can be defined as the spirit.

This view is not of the self as an isolated individual, but a unique self that lives in relationship to our communities, our environment, and our fundamental and greater nature.

Belonging

Picture a group of people standing in a city park on a summer's morning. They have stopped for a while. They have taken off their shoes, and feel the grass beneath their feet, experiencing the way it presses between their toes and the dew cools their soles. They breathe in the air that surrounds them, air which moves across the whole planet and is breathed by all life on Earth. These people are standing beside oak trees that have experienced 500 years of life evolve and change around them, they have stood in countless storms and sun-filled days. Bees are buzzing around the nearby flower garden, ensuring that life continues for all.

The sun is shining on their faces, as it has shone for billions of years on the evolution of the planet. The wind is gently blowing through their hair, connecting them to the earth's beginnings and the great winds of heat and solar energies that shaped this sun and solar system, and back to the very beginning, to, the great explosions of heat and energy that shaped our galaxy, and the billions of galaxies spinning across the universe.

All of this is connected to these few humans standing in an urban park; they are not part of a separate world, but of a world and universe emerging around and through them. Here, dressed in work clothes, are wild humans who can feel, sense and imagine the depths of themselves standing with the mysterious purpose of existence, and through this experience touch into and creatively express the depths of the Earth and universe. Here stands the Natural Self embodied in our modern world: seeking, curious, and loving our homecoming.

A Living and Flourishing Natural Self: A Personal Cosmology

Here we highlight the fundamental parts of a way of living that leads to the flourishing of a Natural Self, and the relationship to a personal cosmology.

A cosmology is a way to understand and orient ourselves within our world and the universe.

Human beings are filled with wonder, and we feel awe in the, contemplation, sensing, feeling and imagining of who we are and our connections to all things. This wonder and awe can point us to our intricate place in the web of life, and throughout history, human beings have found ways to express and share it with others. Around the fires of our nomadic travels, in caves, in community gatherings, in temples, concerts, galleries, and universities, we share and gather our stories, ideas and creative expressions as a way of exploring these great questions.

These cosmologies often speak of our place amongst the other than human: the animals, the plants, the earth and beyond, to the cosmos of sky, sun, moon and stars. We have built many intricate maps, practices, laws and symbolic places to represent this. In these sacred places and within sacred conversations we continue to find a mysterious depth and a 'whole-ly' connection (the same roots as the word holy) to all things, feeding our deep, soulful inquiry.

In all our cultures we have built cosmologies and stories that offer a way of expressing our thoughts, beliefs, musings and symbols to ourselves, to others and to the whole of nature and mystery. These cosmologies would often have an upper world of transcendent reality, and an underworld of inner depth and earthliness. In modern times many of our sacred practices are founded with the purpose of transcending our primal human place on Earth, rising above nature and seeking a sense of purity' as part of this process. The downward, inscendant traditions of Earth-based cultures have been dismissed as at best irrelevant, and at worst, evil.

We have embraced a new story of our place in time, on the earth and in the universe – this is the modern 21st century science story, this has given us a new story and cosmology and, as Brian Swimme and Mary Evelyn Tucker say, "…this story has the power to awaken us more deeply to who we are…the Universe reflecting on itself' (4).

This book sets out to help us explore some of the key questions that we have asked as humans throughout history. *Who am I, and what is my place in the web of all things? What does it mean to be a natural human being connected to myself and to others, and indigenous to my place on the earth? How am I actually the earth and the cosmos reflecting upon themselves?*

We want you to explore your own cosmology, and potentially find within this healing, resources, guidance, and a community of people and a new relationship to the more than human world. Through this, you can enhance the development of your Natural Self and continue to deepen your journey as a Global Indigenous human, finding ways to live well with yourself, each other and the wild earth – in short, to come back home.

A Natural Self knows the world fully and trusts ecological wisdom.

Science comes from the Latin word to know and in modern times our understanding of the truth has been primarily limited to the intellectual and rational. This over-reliance on one way of knowing has led to the demise of other faculties that a Natural Self uses to experience life.

These faculties are discussed by Eligio Gallegos who wrote about these in the book, *Animals of the Four Windows* (5). These four windows, also called the windows of knowing, bring alive again the realms of senses, feeling, emotion and imagination alongside the great gifts of our more rational, thinking mind.

Throughout this book we reference these windows and discuss practices that encourage us to know ourselves, each other and the world equally through them.

These windows offer multiple ways of knowing, expressing and embodying the great wisdom inherent in our relationship to the earth and cosmos.

A Natural Self is Earth.

One of the things we often hear is that we live on the earth as if we somehow arrived here! The Natural Self knows that we are Earth, thinking, sensing, feeling, imagining, and dreaming. All other beings on the planet are our companions, and hold the web of ecological health with us.

This human body we inhabit is a part of the greater earth body, and is the result of billions of years of evolution that is intricately woven through our thinking, sensing, feeling and imagining. With this at the forefront, we come back to body-based practices that inform our lives and the development of a Natural Self.

Coming back to our roots resources us in our development and maturation as humans. A deeper relationship to our body, the earth body, can help us remember we are all indigenous to this planet and feel a deep sense of belonging within this 'home'.

A Natural Self is connected to the wellspring of creativity.

The forces that created life are still a deep mystery – our personal creation remains steeped in so many unanswerable questions, such as *why here, why now, why this family, this story?*

We arise in a constellation of so many intersecting processes; within us all is a deep well of creativity that connects to these mysterious depths, which we have found ways to express through art, music, words, dance and craft. A Natural Self offers creativity and a creative life without expectations of ego-fulfillment or financial reward; rather, this is offered as an articulation of our depths, our healing, our human journey and our deep expression of the rhythms, beauty and power of the wild earth and the cosmos.

A Natural Self understands its ancestry and honours the ones yet to come.

If we are to trace our evolution, we must look to the beginning of the universe, a 13.8 billion year journey that Brian Swimme and Mary Evelyn Tucker beautifully illustrate in *Journey of the Universe* (4). From this new science story we can know our ancestry not just within human history, but to galaxies, stars, rocks, fish, mammals, apes and hominins.

This new understanding of ourselves allows us to see that we are part of a generative process and a continuous evolutionary wave that extends far into the future of those yet to come. There is a need to honour and respect our ancestry, and be conscious of what we are offering to the ones yet to come.

A Natural Self seeks to live in an Earth-focused community.

Across the world, new models for the building of Earth-focused communities are emerging. The development of personal support networks and healthy human connections are vital if we are to sustain a way of living that allows a Natural Self to flourish.

Given that most of us are living in urban environments, there are many challenges and opportunities for creative action. The fundamental values that underpin this community development are the respect and honouring of the individual, the human community and the more than human world, and the reciprocal nature of these relationships.

A Natural Self is connected to place and to the local Earth community.

The needs and dreams of our self and our human communities need to be woven into the land that we inhabit.

Within this land is the local Earth community: the animals, plants, soil, rocks and others that can be incorporated into any way of living we choose. This can be done both in practical ways, with re-wilding and sustainability, and in other ways, such as creative, educational, ritual, ceremonial, and nature-connection practices that acknowledge the presence of these others, their support and their wise guidance.

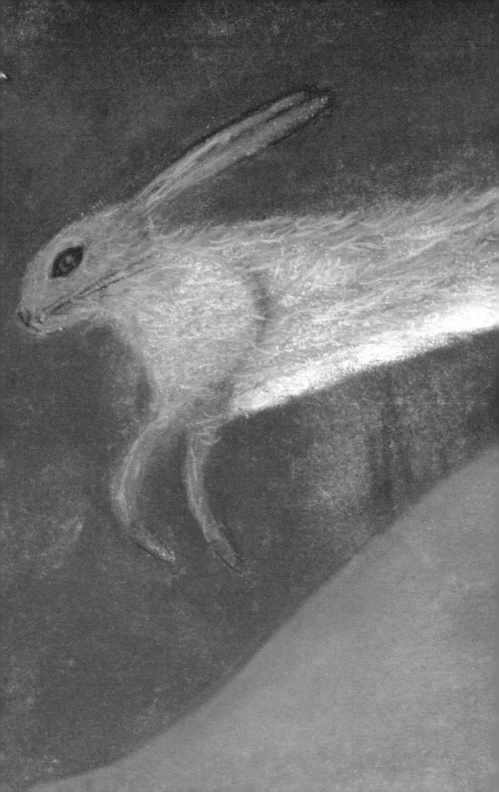

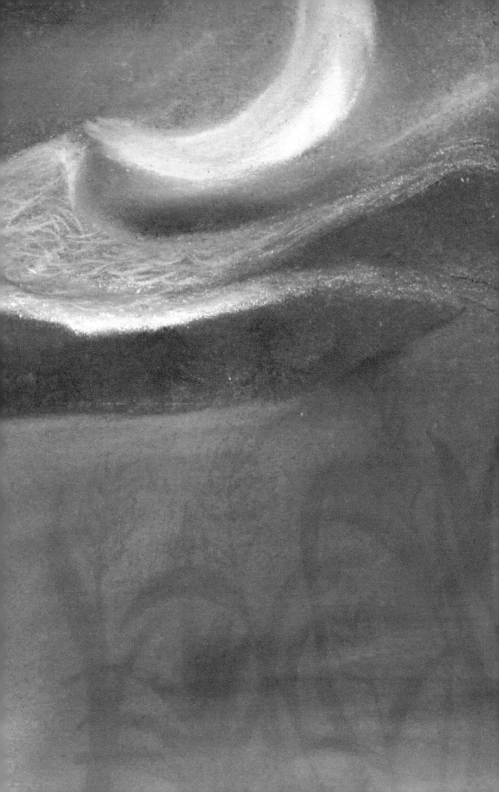

Section 3

The Natural Self Approach

We have developed this book to help deepen your connection with yourself, each other and the natural world. Through these new ideas, practices and support you will be able to develop deep holistic wellness, a rooted resilience, and find ways of living in harmony with your deeper purpose as a human on this earth. As shown in the Natural Self model (*Figure. 1*) we see our self as an interdependent, emerging self, deeply interconnected within our mind, body, and soul, with each other, the world, and the cosmos.

Our approach to developing your Natural Self is founded on eight key aspects (*see Figure 2 page 29*).

Helping You Develop a New Narrative

Through reflection on your self and your ways of living, we encourage you to live by a story founded on the vital parts that help a Natural Self flourish. This story is a narrative informed by your healing journey, your cultivation of wholeness and the deepening of your connection to your inner and greater nature. This narrative is the background to your way of living; it informs your self-discovery or lack of this, your development, your work, other offerings, creativity, relationships and the community you develop.

Highlighting the work of Brian Swimme and Mary Evelyn Tucker, we encourage you to reflect on the universe story, which incorporates the Earth, life and human story. All of us will weave this in different ways, and integrate it with the unique personal, collective, mysterious and mytho-poetic stories of our life. This is an ongoing journey of discovery that will inform your way of living and the development of your Natural Self.

Earth Body Practice

In our approach, we encourage further connection to your body, which we know is deeply and intricately connected to the greater body of Earth, and through this, to the cosmos. The sensitive and feeling nature of our bodies has been overshadowed by a dependency on rational thought and intellect in the attempt to figure life out and/or make it safe.

By deepening into our body, we find the wisdom inherent there, and connect into an inner nature that is fundamentally a part of the wild earth. From this inner wild and primal space, we can find resources and guidance that were long-lost in our over-dependence on the rational mind.

Wild Mind Map of the Psyche

When we look at the Natural Self (*Figure 1 page 18*), the depths and possible expansions of being human are vast. How can we navigate this when we have lost so much of our nature-based cultural traditions, guidance, and support?

We use the 'Wild Mind Map of the Psyche', as developed by Animas Valley Institute and Bill Plotkin (*Ref: 8*). This map integrates thirty-five years of experience, learning and wisdom from working within nature; it shows us how we can come into a resourceful relationship with the vastness of Earth and the cosmos, and look into each direction for healing, facets of wholeness, and our connection to our deep, mysterious inner nature (soul) and expansive outer nature (spirit).

The Map integrates modern depth psychology and pan-cultural nature-based methods, to bring us into a new Indigenous connection in our modern world. Our Natural Self approach weaves this map into our work as a navigation tool and guide, for our healing, cultivation of wholeness, and connection to soul and spirit.

Council and Mentoring

Council is the gathering of a community and can have many intentions. We bring council into our Natural Self approach as a way of sharing our heart, our creativity and our deep imagination. This sharing arises from a reciprocal relationship to ourselves, each other, and the natural world which informs all of the council processes. It is a way of helping to build a more Indigenous community that brings Earth-based practices back to the very heart of culture.

Being held by a community is also vital, given the lack of elders, wise leaders, and the need to once again build communities that hold us in our transitions and maturation. Being mentored and supported within this community is crucial if we are to come into the fullness of our Natural Self, and our approach looks for ways that this support can be incorporated into your life.

Reflection and Mirroring

To be seen is to belong, and in being seen it is important that we hear, sense and feel the reflections of our wholeness – that we are more than a small cog in a giant machine but a Natural Self, alive and creative, wise and mysterious. Our approach incorporates reflection and mirroring throughout so that the amazing truth of our being human is shown. This reflection is not only from other people, but through your own self-reflection, and through the reflection of the natural world as the reciprocal relationship it is. This can lead to a sense of participation with the Earth and its ever-changing and evolving community.

Creative Nature

Finding ways of connecting, honouring and expressing our inherent creative nature and connection to the deep Well Spring of creation itself is a core element of our approach. We work with poetry, writing, art, music, dance, craft, and drama, to encourage the sacred expression of who we are through our creative connections to ourselves each other and the deep Well Spring of the earth and the cosmos.
Through this creation and expression it is possible to find deep healing, cultivate untapped resources, and touch into the mysteries of who we are in connection to the rest of nature.

Nature-based Meditation and Mindfulness

Mindfulness is an ancient practice and is a natural part of our human experience. There are many traditions that look at meditation and mindfulness within natural environments as a way to connect to something greater than us, and to the depths of our being.

Nature-based mindfulness is also a method that leads to deep relaxation, and is a way that we can encourage self-care in our often stressful and busy lives. As part of our Natural Self approach, we encourage a range of nature-based practices that will encourage a state of mindfulness, present-centredness, meditation and conscious living.

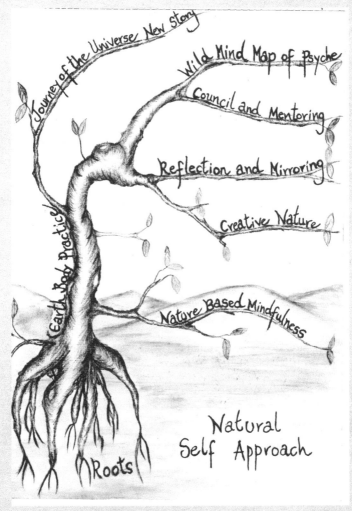

Journey of the Universe New Story

Wild Mind Map of Psyche

Council and Mentoring

Reflection and Mirroring

Creative Nature

Earth Body Practice

Nature Based Mindfulness

Natural Self Approach

Roots

Figure 2

Roots

We are all born out of mystery into a unique personal story, a particular place and time. Our roots reach into family, background, culture and the place, or places, we are born into. They stretch into our ancestry and our shared human emergence and deeper still into our beginnings in animal, plants and down into the emergence of cells and life itself. In the very heart of the Earth we touch the primal substance that formed us and continues to shape us. By giving attention to these roots much emerges, pain, deep emotion, challenge, healing, growth, resources, new story, development, awe, love, energy, evolution, soul all combining to form the soil and bedrock of an authentic, passionate, connected and grounded life.

Section 4

Preparation and Simplification

Our lives are now so full of information, discussion, and entertainment, that there can be limited time – or desire – for our Natural Self to be nourished through a connection to nature.

One way that you might prepare for the practices that follow is to switch off the devices that hold your attention. It is up to you what you decide; it might be for a time during practice, or for a longer period, or even forever with some devices.

The more time given over to relaxation, spaciousness, feeling into your depths, into your heart, mindfulness, and into your nature based connections, the more your Natural Self can emerge.

Start this journal and begin to capture your journey.

At the back of this book, and within the practices, you will find space for self-reflection and creativity. This is intended to help you integrate your experiences, as it is a very useful way of capturing what is emerging for you in the discovery of your Natural Self. We encourage creative expression through drawing, art, poetry, stories etc., so that the symbolic and mythic experience of the reciprocal relationship with nature can be expressed.

Places of Practice

A place of practice is important to establish – there may be a combination of places that are available to you, or you may be more restricted. Not to worry – even the city has the wild sky above, and this may be just right for you.

Otherwise, there are three main areas to practice regularly:-

- A garden
- A park
- A wilder space

Section 5

10 Practices That Can Support You

1. Remembering Our Connections and Nature Based Mindfulness

2. Earth Body, Felt Sense

3. Deeper Conversation – Sit Spot

4. Resources – the Four Directions

5. Threshold and Deep Imagination

6. Welcoming the Dark and the Unbidden

7. Wandering and the Calling

8. Longing and the Trembling Heart

9. Integrating the practices; living as your Natural Self

10. Gratitude for a Reciprocal Relationship

1. Remembering Our Connections and Being Mindful in Nature

Being mindful is taking your attention to what is happening in this moment arising through the four windows of knowing, thinking, sensing, feeling and imagining. It is also the awareness of what we are doing in our tasks, movement or play. It can lead to something called present-centredness, where we are fully present in the moment and to what is happening within and without.

Immerse yourself in this practice whenever and wherever you can. When walking to work, take notice of the sky. In the passenger seat in a car or bus, and stuck in a traffic jam, look at the trees by the motorway. While walking through a park, stop and listen, look, feel, and touch the earth, trees' and plants.

Nature Based Mindfulness

Find a place in your garden, park or wilder nature; somewhere that you are comfortable and can spend a few minutes, or longer, to allow yourself to begin to drop into your connection. Take a few minutes to arrive in that place.

Begin by noticing your breath and using your senses. Take some time, maybe with your eyes closed, to tune into your body and your senses, noticing the sounds that surround you, perhaps further away, perhaps closer by; tune into any sense of touch – of the sun or the wind in your hair, or touching the ground, trees, and plants; into the sense of smell, of the air and the land, coming to the sense of sight.

Whatever it is, stay with it in this mindful way, whether it is the wind on your face, the rain on your head, or the sound of the wind.

Being Wildly Mindful

We know that often the wild is associated with excitement, noise, running around, and being outrageous. Watch the wild animals – many spend a lot of time very still and quiet. We have that wild centre in our own Natural Self, and a deep, inner place of stillness and relaxation.

Journal: Write about your experience of being mindful in nature, what did you notice, feel, sense. Perhaps you can draw a moment that came.

Wild Stillness

There is the place, deep in forest green,
not moving as winds howl at the edges,
only the silence waiting for my first approach.

I saw the rock and sat,
watching the fluorescence of green, mossy banks
having time for the touch of grass;
the sound of a leaf dropping.

How this green jewel had waited, patient in its fullness,
luminosity shining out in darkest winter day, calling for my return.

I sat and sensed alert, quiet in easy breath, wondering what threading vine
brought me here.
Then all moved.

For the deer approached with soundless tip toe touch,

Gentle hooves on pine needle beds.

It stopped and looked into the dark, where something seemed to call in silence,
ears moved, eyes fixed.

My heart was beating.
My chest gentle in breathless pulse.
My body held in steady poise.

Wild mind,
Wild stillness.

A Natural Self: Earth body, Open heart, Clear mind.

2. Earth Body, Felt Sense

Remembering our Earth body is a key to coming into our senses and into connection with our own Natural Self.

Let yourself feel the free, unconditioned wild being that you are – an Earth body that wanders through the land, playful, sensuous and present, connected to the land, and at one with it. Remember the place of wild stillness as well. Perhaps there is a sense of the wild child who splashes in mud and climbs trees, moving this wild Earth body within the land, being in a reciprocal relationship with wind, animals, birds, trees and plants, and moving with them.

There is a real feeling of relief in coming into our wildness when we give ourselves permission. It is so good to let ourselves be really absorbed by our senses and the movement of our bodies. We have watched many people in our work begin this journey with a sense of uncertainty and shame, as we have been so shamed in our culture, so don't be surprised if you feel self-conscious or shy.

It is so important to start, and stepping outside of your comfort zone may be a real challenge, but all who we have worked with have appreciated how much it helped them to connect to their Natural Self.

Journal: How do you feel in your body, what ways do you remember being free and wild in nature? How does your body connect to the greater earth body?

Earth Body

In this city the reflection of it all,
wind in hair and branches,
clouds moving across a sunrise eye,
and song birds calling from my throat.

See the river below, how the slow watery depths and rushing rapids move my
blood,
heart pumping wild through veins of busy streets.

My feet are planted in an avenue of trees and my hair tousled by the breathing
breeze of pigeons.
I am reaching up rooted to Earth, spirit to soul.
The hills rest across my easing heart,
and the night of stars reminds me of exploding truths, that my mind can only
remember
when silence finally comes.

See it all,
Feel it all,
Be it all
Before you hear the final call.

A Natural Self: Mirrored by all of nature.

3. Deeper Conversation – Sit-Spot, Nook

To get to know a place is to get to know ourselves. A sit spot is a practice that offers a way of becoming intimate with a place over a longer period of time. To go back to the same spot on a regular basis creates time for you to experience the reciprocal relationship, and how this supports you in the discovery of your Natural Self.

You may find somewhere close to you, in your garden, or it may be somewhere you walk to. The intention is to find a natural space, and build your relationship with it. Get to know who lives there, trying not to disturb any creatures' homes. Introduce yourself to this place, and allow it to show itself to you.

You may stay for minutes, hours, or longer. You might, on occasions, stay overnight and experience the place in darkness; in the context of the dark, the stars, and the moon will change the narrative, and bring in other aspects of the relationship. Being there throughout the different seasons will show you other dimensions and further deepen your intimacy.

To be in this conversation with the natural world is vital, as our Natural Self knows that we are shaped, grown and initiated by it. We often look towards each other for guidance and support, and as we further deepen our Indigenous connections, we also remember that the more that human is longing for us to come home too.

Journal: keep a creative log of your experiences in your sit spot, what threads do you notice, how does it change over time and what words, images or sensations are present for you there.

Conversations

How the bee is called full-headed, buzz-backed to the place where it can always worship the true calling of its wild soul.

How it marks the way and finds the way, with reverence to the mystery of its wisdom.

The place marked as altar green sending its wild heart beating with the sight of daisies, clover heads and...
Trembling at the beauty, the colours, the fragrance of the land.

Headlong, heart full, body blasted to fly into the heart of flowery delights, sinking deeply into true purpose.

Mark the time, bow down to the beauty of it all; swim in mystery.

Collect the bones of ancestors, dreams of wild child, majesty of stars.

Collect them all and set them down to your sacred space, a sacred place.

There reach for what the symbols point towards and stop and sit, and stop and sit.

Getting Lost At Last

To wander is, at last, to risk getting lost
And not knowing the way relieves the tiresome burden I carry to some other place.

The direction is always a sense, knowing that just over there, in the corner of this wilder place, is where I must go.
There I can find a threading vine that leads to some other thicket
And in that place once again risk getting even more lost.

To stay uncomfortable but moved,
Not knowing if the way the beauty of the butterfly shapes should be followed,

Or if that voice in the wind is what I should listen to in the other conversation.

For how can I ever know what the unknown way is showing?
I can only allow the feeling of adventure to come
And to wander with no purpose,
Bringing blessed relief
And sweet simple gifts

Bringing me back, to this right place in the heart of all things.

4. Resources – the Four Directions

Each of the cardinal directions has its own energy which we can evoke or call on, and these energies, or deep structural patterns, are constantly available to us. This is a way in which we can resource ourselves whilst developing and maturing our Natural Self. Calling in the Directions is a practice that has been used across cultures for thousands of years. We work with Bill Plotkins' *Wild Mind Map of the Psyche*, which is a powerful and accessible way to cultivate the archetypal resources we need to navigate the journey of our Natural Self.

You can begin in any of the directions; here we will begin in the North. We may imagine or create a circle, and, speaking out loud, we can call in the North. This is the generative adult, the one of us that can take care of what it is needed both for self and others, the one who makes things happen, and who acts on behalf of the world in the right way, the one of us that can listen to what's being asked of us, and is willing to act from a generous and loving place.

We then turn to the East, and call on the Sage of us, the wise fool, the innocent one; the one that sees each day afresh, and can hold the bigger picture and vision. We can also remember to keep some humour, and develop our lightness. The feeling of ascending, as the sun does each day in the East, is a guide who helps us to maintain the spirit of the world and remember we are all part of a whole.

Turning to the South, we evoke our wild, embodied, sensual, emotional being; the one of us that knows we belong to a place, the one who knows we are part of the web of life and all beings; the one that welcomes all feelings, and is delighted by the capacity to be in our wild human body.

Finally we come to the West, the return to the soil, the inscendance to the unknown, the decomposition, the decay; to remembering that we have a relationship with death as much as we do with life that all goes back to the soil, and from which the deep, creative, imaginative mysteries of life can emerge. In the west we can call on the muse or the inner beloved as guides to express the deeper, darker forces of our nature.

Journal: Write from each direction, how would the North write or draw, what would this direction say to you? Go around each direction and let the direction have a voice or expression through you.

All Around

I cannot rest, I cannot sleep, and I have heard that the medicine I need is
always just around me,
if only I could see,
trust to look
where the silhouette pointing branch dares me to,
There after sun has set, a root hollow, open in darkness of depths, offering a
hand of mystery that beckons to be taken.

I turn away and stand with North Star bright, remembering that even one of
these has to die for me to be alive
for life to grow
forged in that furnace of love.

The distant hint of dawn arising catches me, faint line of orange, stars rushing
back to en-darken
My body knows the moon high above is pulling, and feels the quickening of my
heart, the rushing of blood
There is nowhere to go to find the healing and the truth
My becoming is the medicine.

5. Threshold and Deep Imagination

A threshold is one way of entering a different state and a sense of the otherworldly; we offer this practice as a way to access a shift of consciousness. Through a threshold we can move from an everyday state of consciousness, in order to hear or open up to our experience of the world in a new, alternative way.

The four windows of knowing discussed earlier are vital ways that we can access this shift, stretching out the senses, dropping into the deep, feeling heart of our wild body and the earth, seeing ourselves and the other than human community through the imagination. Some people might like to take a drum or other instrument, dance with the land, or drop into their animal body.

Find a place in nature that you want to wander through. You can make a threshold in your imagination, or you can take a couple of sticks and lay them in front of you. There may be a natural threshold where two trees appear. When you step over the threshold you are leaving your everyday life and opening up, becoming available to the other world. You will wander and feel what your body, emotions, and imagination are guiding you to.

You might feel yourself called to a particular place or being; you might know this is a place important to you as your heart begins to tremble; you may feel terrified as well as excited. You may feel repulsed as well as curious. You may allow these more unusual feelings to guide you. Or you may cross the threshold with a particular being or facet of your self in mind, to meet, to have a conversation with and get to know more deeply.

You might find that, having called in the directions over a period of time, you can sense where you are out of balance and that you need to cultivate an aspect of your resources. Cross the threshold to evoke this and go for a walk, sit in council or find a spot in nature that is a mirror of what you need - being mindful that this is a reciprocal relationship.

Stay for as long as it takes, and then prepare to leave, bringing back whatever was offered. As you leave, remember to close the threshold behind you. This is a powerful and beautiful practice and often opens up to the unbidden and emergent parts of us.

Journal: Reflect on what happens when you step through a threshold and find a different state of consciousness. Perhaps write this poetically or draw images. Reflect and mirror what you meet in this other place?

Threshold

I always knew this place was here, waiting,
Even on the most tedious day.
Even when the dark mists of foggy fumes drifted past me at the bus stop as I
rushed headlong, heart closed to work.
I knew somewhere deep inside, that
Just past the housing estate, on the corner near the pub.
An old Victorian gate, wrought rust,
Ivy woven.
Tangled to an impenetrable dark place,
here was the way in to something else.
Even though I was not sure if the sounds that echoed behind really were the
noise of the wild places that so ached inside.
I knew my wanders in wondering space had brought me here.

And through the trembling of my heart I knew this was the way.

A Natural Self: Welcomes the dark and unknown.

6. Welcoming the Dark and the Unbidden

The dark has been made evil and wrong in our society. Growing up, we may have been told that nasty, dangerous creatures will come out of the dark and get us, and so we grow up terrified of it, when in fact the dark is a rich, fecund place, full of possibilities and creativity. What goes on beneath the surface of the earth, that which is unseen, is essential. The rich, dark soil is full of life, full of complex networks that are supporting and birthing all kinds of wonders. Then, there's the 96% of darkness that makes up the universe: the dark matter and dark energy that scientists have located, and of course, there is our own dark nature that, if we get to know it, may become a guide and a teacher.

To sit with the dark, to talk to the dark, and tell it our deepest longing; to actively and consciously invite the dark; to welcome it; to sit in the unknown; to allow again the unbidden; to fall into the descent time is to see things again from another place.

We may have a conversation with death and dying, as we all return to the soil eventually. This practice can help cultivate our development of our Natural Self; sitting with these powerful forces of the unknown, dark, decay and death, we can develop a new relationship with ourselves and life again.

Journal: After spending time in the dark, write about what you meet being in the dark, what aspects of yourself or the more than human world meet you? Explore how you can be with what emerges and write, paint, draw, sculpt ways of representing this.

For me this night is long and sweet.

The Night is always about to start,
And I know that what I feel in darkness moves close,
Sweet shade of dread and wonder,
What is it that you see? When the dark moon closes its eye ·
And night draws deep, the path lost in the undergrowth weaves.

Strange sounds that call to the shadows of the trees and hills,
And deeper wells of water echo, with the gentle splashes of weeping ones

It is time for those that do their work at night to rustle forth beside me,
slither and crawl in leafy rot
For they know that all decay is but the shimmer of a new born,
slight and quick to life,
in wombs of slime and mold.

For me this night is long,
my mind demented, stretched to the edges of the mystery.
allowing owls and moths to fly across my shadow land.
See the silhouettes of leafless trees, grasp stars and take their light.
The dark moons stare unblinking and unseen.

For me this night is long and sweet, and I am lost and found again. And I am lost
and found again.

A Natural Self: Wandering and wondering.

7. Wandering and the Calling

In modern living, many have forgotten how to be free and wander in nature - to move without objectives and plans, and instead be in present relationship to our body and the earth.

Go out to a garden, park or wilder nature, pass through a threshold and wander without intention – nowhere to go in particular, just allowing yourself to follow your body's senses or your own intuition.

Wandering is free of the busy thinking that you need to get somewhere and achieve something, going so many miles, or climbing that mountain, having to conquer something. By moving or walking without intention, you are developing and deepening your relationship to the moment and to what is actually there.

This again takes practice, and you may feel very disorientated. It is the physical preparation for letting go of old patterns and deepening into intuitive listening, moving away from your thinking of where you should be going and allowing your other senses to guide and inform you.

You may find yourself drawn to a particular place, or enticed there. It might feel both terrifying and alluring to approach this place. In cultivating our Natural Self we can find the courage to face that which brings fear, mirrored in nature – this may be a thread to follow, and not to turn away from.

When we talk about being called, we are tuning in to this deeper body, feeling, and sensing experience. It may be the way the light is falling on a spot in the woodland; it might be that you feel so totally at one in this place, like it is a good place to rest forever; it might not make any sense to be with this place.

Journal: What might you offer to this place as a poem? You could tell it your story, or invite the place to tell you its own. Write these down. Perhaps draw the story of your wonder like a mythic journey.

Wandering

To wander is to risk getting lost and then be fully found,
Not knowing the way or the time it will take
'But' I cry 'I can't do that, not me, not now'
To stay with this edge of unknown, knowing.
Where is up and where is down and how to get to where I want?

For only in this moments step can I feel a blessed relief,
Body moved and mind relaxed
Yielding to the peaceful stretch of horizons opening in this way and that,
Shrouds unveiling the mystery of it all.
Bringing me back, to this place right now,
within the heart of all things striding forth.

8. Longing and the Trembling Heart

It would seem that there is always a sense of our deepest longing, our yearning, and the ache for who we truly are. It would also seem that being alone with nature evokes this, and can fill us with grief and deep love. Attention is not given to feeling and being with our deeper awareness through our body, and therefore we learn to be in our feelings in a much more superficial way. We begin to pathologies these deeper experiences, and try to deny ourselves who and what we were born to be. Of course, it can feel counter-cultural to go after our deep grief, allow ourselves to be cracked open by the sheer beauty of a place, or fall in love what we are deeply longing to be in the world. To deepen into your Natural Self we are encouraging you to do exactly this: to follow what makes your heart trembles with its own knowing, to feel the deep longing, and to follow where and what that leads you to. This is a practice for us to grow and allow the power of our very being to emerge again.

The world needs us to come alive, to be our full Natural Self.

Journal: Write or draw your deepest longing, how do you know this, how do you feel this. Reflect on how nature mirrors this to you?

The Beloved

The morning light is murmuring its soft dreamings to me
life can't wait, it whispers, the stars are fading but will always return.
in the garden the trees are bowing in the wind, new leaves rushing to meet
spring sun.

I know you lie awake under that dark Oak, waiting for me or for the dawn to end
or maybe I don't know what the mystery is of you.

I do know the earth has spun in love around the sun and we have been together
perhaps forever or maybe never.
that movement of the trees outside shows we have always sought each other,
an eternity of seeking, since wind began blowing stars around the galaxies,
since all the seas crashed on distant planet shores we have longed for each
other.

And as long as the stars rise in the evening we can never come together.
I know we lit a fire.
that fire that burns between us still brings the light and sends the shadows
dancing on the cliff dunes.
our wild hearts beating with the pounding sea.
The soft drift wood burning so well, full of stars.

I knew as I know now that this was the end and the beginning of me.
I am not here anymore but with you dancing in the light and shadows waiting for
the stars to return. knowing that when they do we must part again.

A Natural Self: An intricate part of the Earth community.

9. Integrating the practices; living as your Natural Self

All of the above practices are ways in which you can cultivate your resources to assist you in living a more balanced life. In this journey you will find healing and resources of wholeness, and will meet the mysterious realm of the soul, where your deepest purpose and place are.

Like any landscape that has been deeply wounded, it takes time to recover and begin to rebalance, and to find a way to cultivate life again. Our internal scape, our own wilderness, needs to be given time to recover, and to cultivate the wholeness needed so that we can become our Natural Self once again.

To return to our community and to bring the gifts that only we can offer, is what the world is longing for. Finding ways in which you can offer this in your life and embody yourself fully is an ongoing and deepening pract ice of living.

Take time in nature to be with your healing journey noticing how the land can support you in this. What does it reflect and how can the wholeness of nature help you with your fragmentation? Take time to also acknowledge the resources that are developing in you, and to find ways of being within the deep mystery of a mytho-poetic encounter with your soul, such as a name called to you, an image that haunts you, or a felt sense of something mysterious in your sit spot. How can you bring this all back to serve yourself, your community and the greater Earth community.

Journal: Reflect on your healing journey and how this is present in your life at this time. What are the main resources you need to cultivate to support you and to help you flourish? Is there an image, a name, a mysterious encounter that points to something soulful in you?

What's in a Name?

It may seem that we have only one name,
When it is called, all the earth comes to attention and knows that we have heard
the truth of what we have to do.
This name, that shudders us in fear, a terror of losing the most precious ones of
us
Just as they are found.
A name that haunts us in our dreams and comes knocking on the door of our
life, again and again and once more.

And oh confusion! there can seem to be so many names waiting to be called.
Every day another one comes, in the dawn light with the bird singing a song not
heard before, ·
and that leaf shimmers for the first time in the rising sun,
beckoning a word that dances from the image in your heart.

You do know your name.
All around you wild ones call it to you, in newly composed melodies,
dazzling you in the mirrors of their seeing.
Mystery offers you this name,
As a story thread to weave
in a never seen design.

A Natural Self: Communing with the more than human world.

10. Gratitude for a Reciprocal Relationship

Being thankful for the gift of this wild life is a core part of our healing and personal development, and can deeply enhance our sense of connection to the more than human world. Finding ways to be thankful for our lives, and being present on the earth amongst the wonder of nature is a way of us remembering how the earth is always supporting us. Praising the natural world, so that the world is deeply loved and appreciated, is both a reconnection to our external environment and to our inner Natural Self, as we *are* nature.

Go out every day, and find gratitude for the other than human world. Offering an act of music, poetry or movement can be a beautiful way to respond to the others. You may want to say a prayer, or sing praises to the earth, or to the cosmos; any ceremony of gratitude will work well. There is also the opportunity before you eat to acknowledge the offering of the food, and the plants or animals that have given up their life to feed you.

Journal: Write down all the things you are grateful for in your life and in the world around you. Find ways of writing praise and appreciation to the Earth and all that it provides. Perhaps there is one animal or plant that you can focus on for a time.

Gratitude

The air is cold and sharp today
This garden has not been tended to in a while,
Old terracotta pots have begun to decay
And I feel the eyes of the green man you hung so long ago peering through

He watches as I dig and
I dig so deep
With my hands in this soil, the earthy smell turns into fragrances
that fill me with memories of arrival here
Lavender, mint, marjoram
I am full of sensing here
A warmth and sadness fills my heart
I wonder how long will I know this piece of land
How many years shall I see you cherry blossom tree
Explode into the beauty that you are
Your soft pink petals scattering the lawn once you are done
When will I be done here, here on this land, how long will I know you.

An in that moment deep gratitude,
Deep praise
Deep love
How you hold me in your heart.

Section 6

Stepping further into your life.

We have offered you some ways to reengage, reconnect and remember. We know that this is a journey, probably one of a life time, and we know that there is a cycle to your practice and a rhythm to the way that you engage.

Now that you have worked with the ten practices, the task is to continue deepening and integrating these into your day-to-day living. Perhaps for now you will continue working with one that stands out more, or a combination, or all of them.

The creation of a community of fellow travelers is also vital to ensure that you have support and insight for the challenges and joys that arise.

A reading list can be found at the end of the book, which offers books that have been an important part of our learning and development. There are also an increasing amount of courses, retreats, community services etc. to engage with if you wish to develop your Natural Self further.

We know we could not have done this without the support of all the fellow wondering people we met along the way, and of course, the more than human beings that have supported and guided us.

We wish you well, and send wild blessings from the depths.

Together

When it all weaves like entwining vines

The rising of the daffodils in spring from the dark, cool soil.

Ladybirds in windowsills waking to the warmth.

The bees beginning the honey dance and touching again the petals of the wild flowers.

Without the one how can the other be

Without the other there is no one.

The wild storm clears the ground for all,

the sea strips away the madness for new sanity to emerge

For if the moon had not shone its wild power on our troubled lands, had it not

been ripped as twin from the heart of the earth then how could the fish walk on

land.

And we look up at the dark sky, the endless drift of milky way only a tiny piece of it all.

And we listen and we feel.

The natural one wonders at itself

Section 7

Journal

A Natural Self: Ancient ways in future paths.

REFERENCES

1. TECHNOLOGY, TRAUMA AND THE WILD: Chellis Glendinning. Article

2. THE DREAM OF THE EARTH: Thomas Berry. Published by Sierra Club Books

3. SOULCRAFT: Bill Plotkin. Published by New World Library

4. JOURNEY OF THE UNIVERSE: Brian Thomas Swimme, Mary Evelyn Tucker
   Published by Yale University Press

5. ANIMALS OF THE FOUR WINDOWS: Eligio Stephen Gallegos. Published by
   Moon Bear Press

Further Reading

Thomas Moore: Care of the Soul

James Hillman: On soul, character and calling: A conversation with James Hillman

Theodore Roszak: The Voice of the Earth

Geneen Marie Haugen: Imagining Earth - Spiritual Ecology Collection: The Cry of
the Earth

Bill Plotkin: Wild Mind, Nature and the Human Soul

Thomas Berry: The Sacred Universe: Earth Spirituality and Religion in the Twenty
First Century

Thomas Berry: Dreamer of the Earth: Anthology

Brian Swimme: The Universe is a Green Dragon, The hidden heart of the Universe, The Universe Story

Jay Griffiths: Wild, an Elemental Journey

Spiritual Ecology: The Cry of the Earth Anthology

Earth has a Soul: C.G. Jung's writing on Nature, Technology and Modern Life.

David Abram: Spell of the Sensuous & Animal Body

Poetry

All the poetry in this book is written by Michéal Connors and Rhonda Brandrick.

There are many other poets to dive into, including the works of Mary Oliver, W B Yeats, Seamus Heaney, Wordsworth, David Whyte, Wendell Berry, Rumi, Maria Rilke, and many more.

ND - #0388 - 270225 - C122 - 210/148/7 - PB - 9781912092642 - Matt Lamination